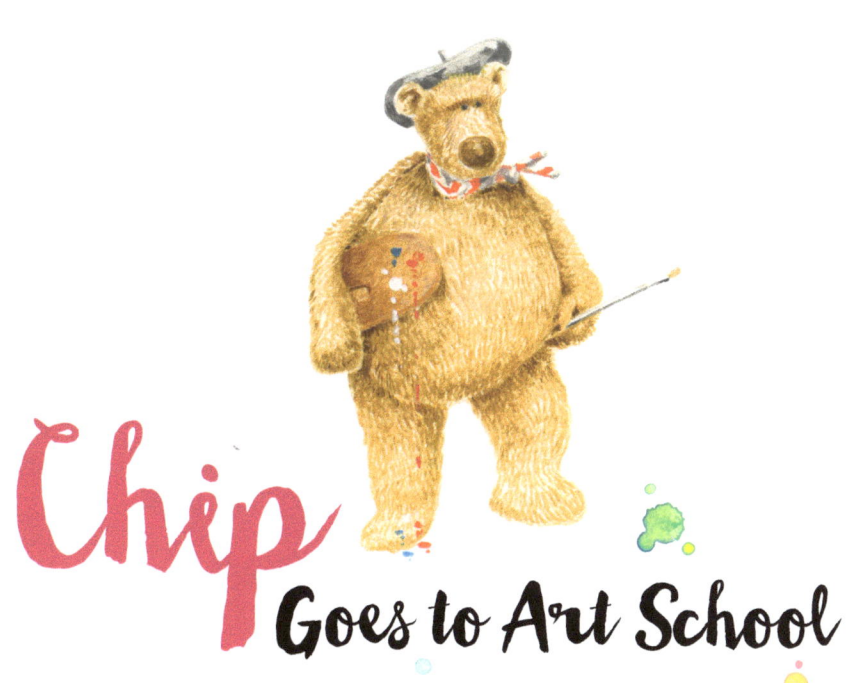

Chip
Goes to Art School

Robert H. Seaman, father of Robin, is a painter, drawer and teacher of drawing.

Robin Hayes, daughter of Robert, is a graphic designer and Chip is Robin's bear.

They all currently live in Keene, NH.

See more of their work at 368Art.com

Images ©2017 Robert H. Seaman

Chip has quite a following on Instagram. Follow his adventures:

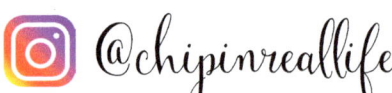 @chipinreallife

Chip Goes to Art School

Chip is from a long line of bears noted for their practical and some might say sensible lines of work. Generations of berry pickers, fishers, and raiders of bird feeders and bee hives, content to patrol their woodsy territories, occasionally exploring the backyards of nearby humans. That sort of life.

Chip, however, had a yearning for something different. He had passionate, creative urges absent in most bears. What to do? Chip decided to go to art school.

And so he did.

He studied, among other subjects, anatomy, portraiture, drawing principles, and of course color theory.

Chip practiced and practiced, and it wasn't long before he was painting portraits and self-portraits, landscapes and still-lifes, works that were abstract, expressionistic, and impressionistic. He even painted realism, surrealism, and unrealism.

He became famous for his virtuosity and range.

Chip's pictures became virtual art-world icons. It's likely you'll recognize many of them in this short but long awaited collection. We'd like to thank the many museums and private collectors who have permitted us to reproduce them.

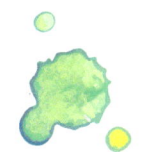

Happy viewing!

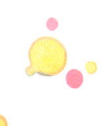

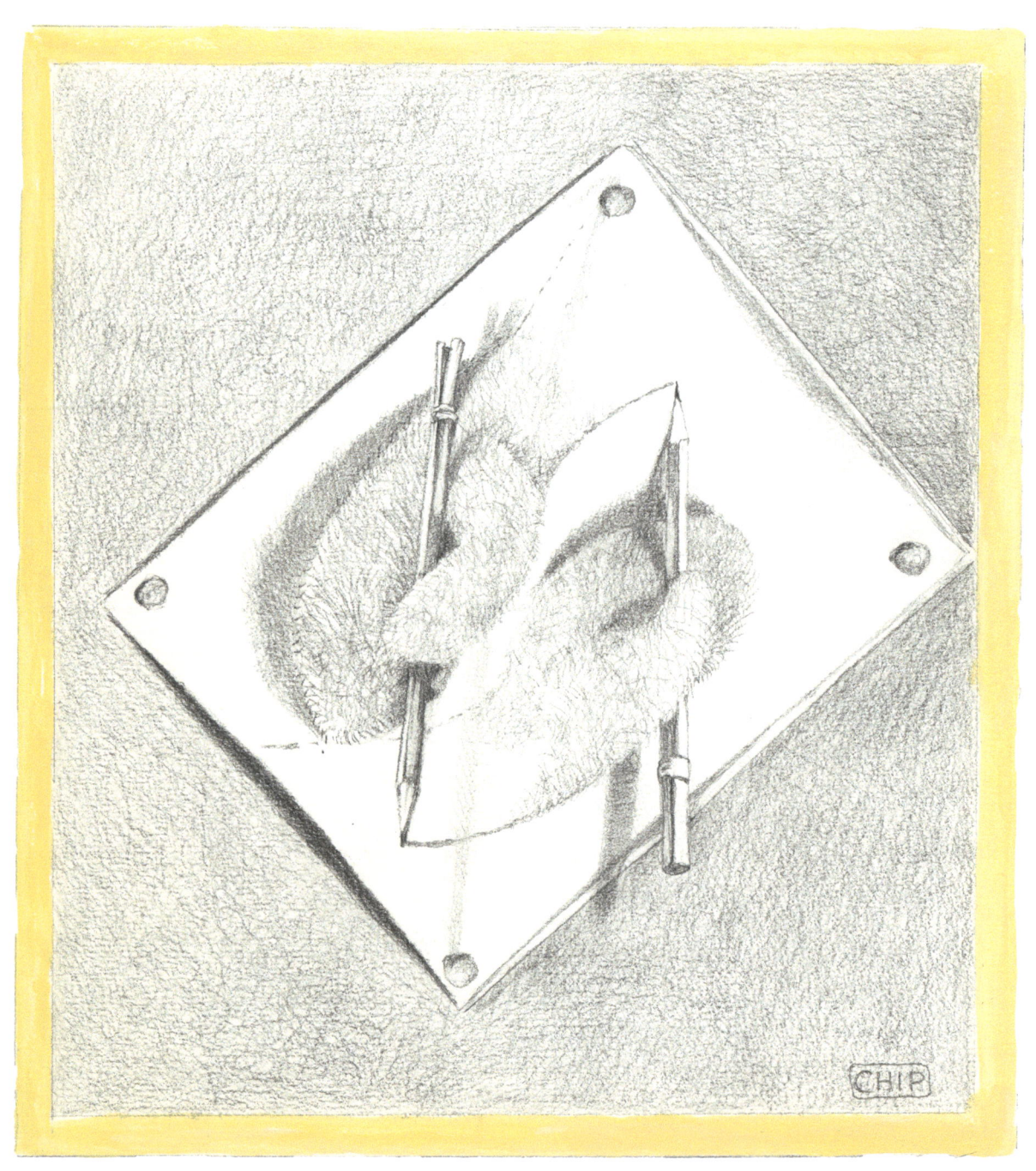

Chip discovered he was a natural at drawing.

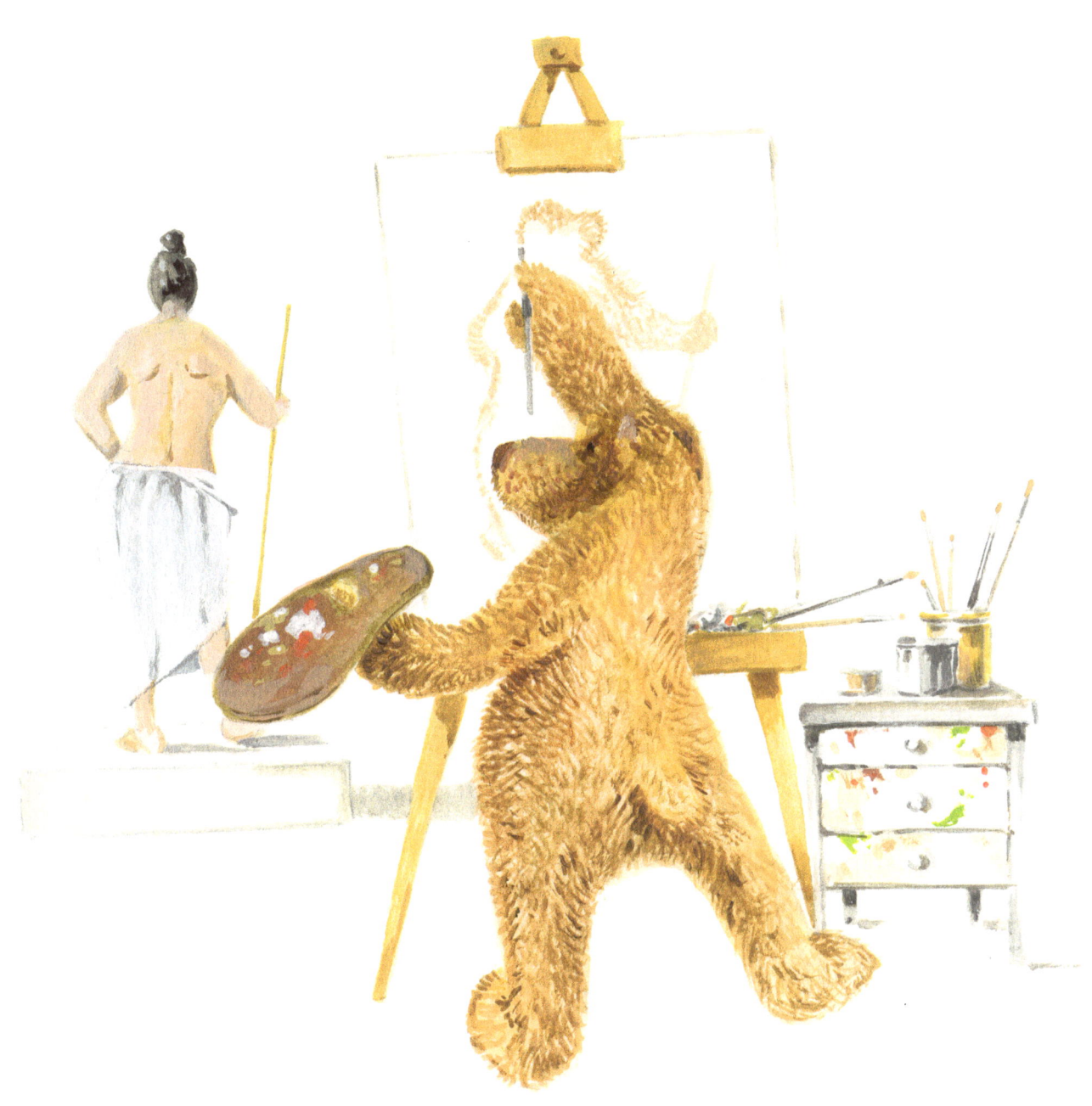

He also loved anatomy studies.

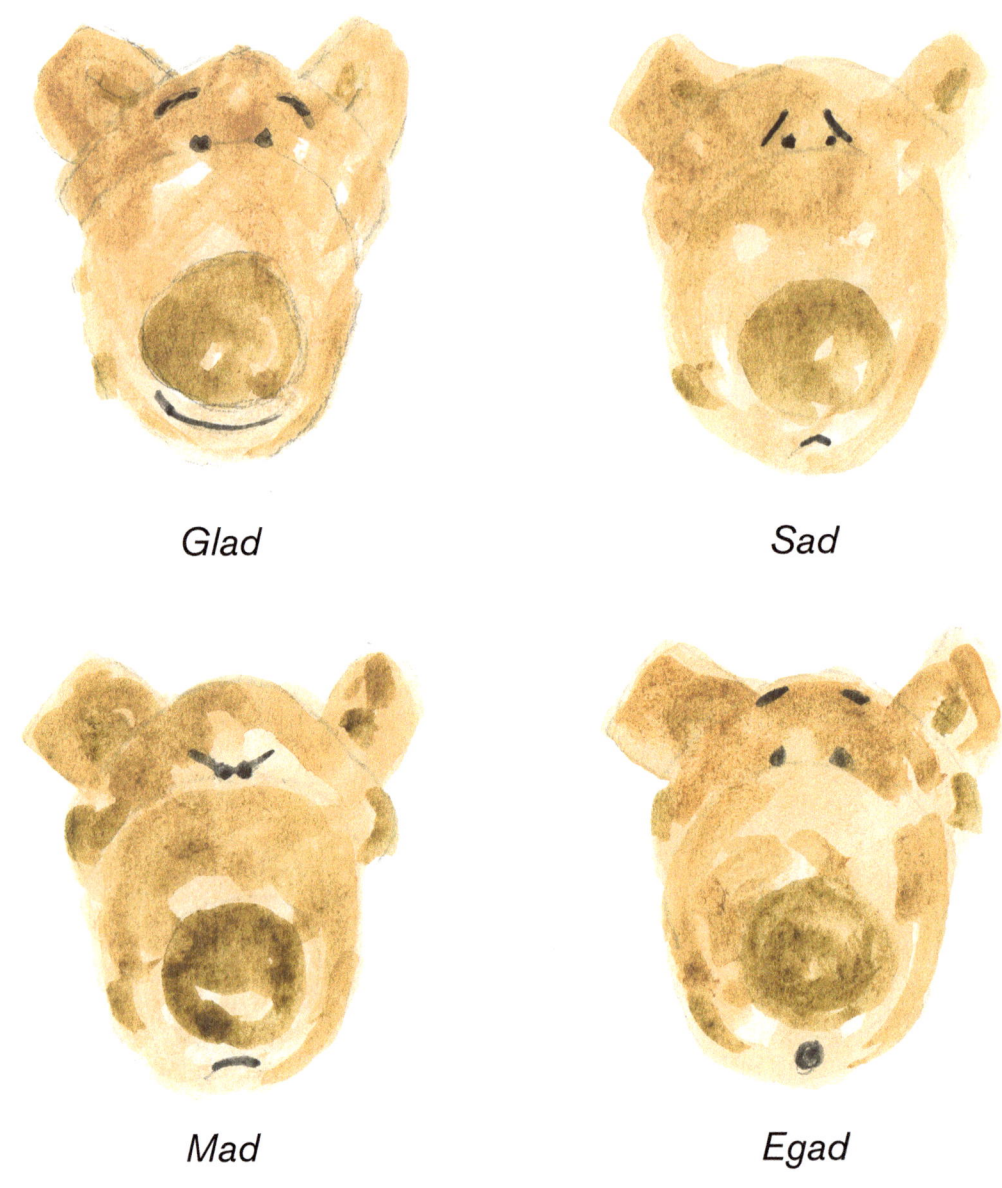

Glad *Sad*

Mad *Egad*

Capturing facial expressions was never a problem.

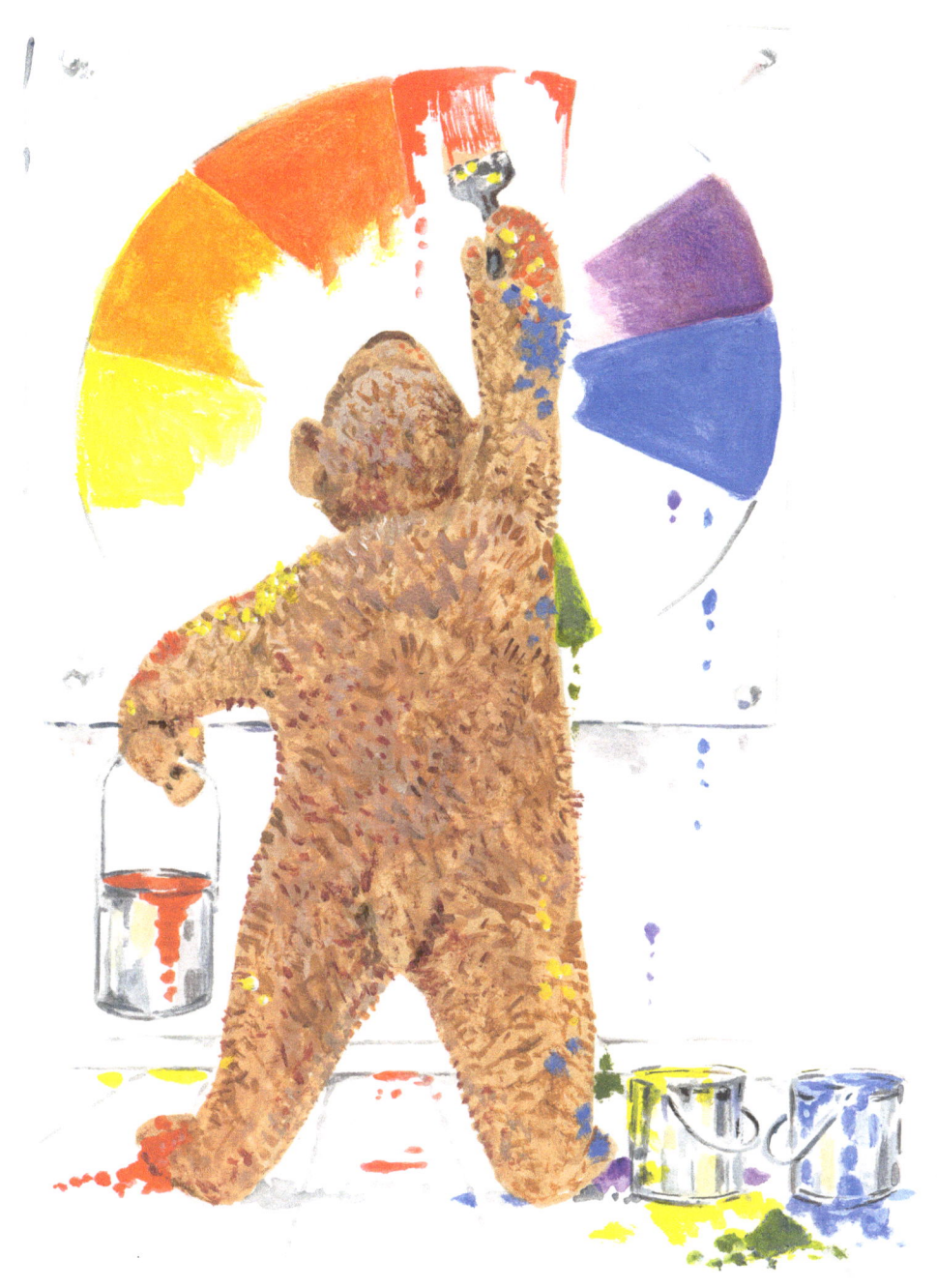

And mastering color theory was like painting by numbers.

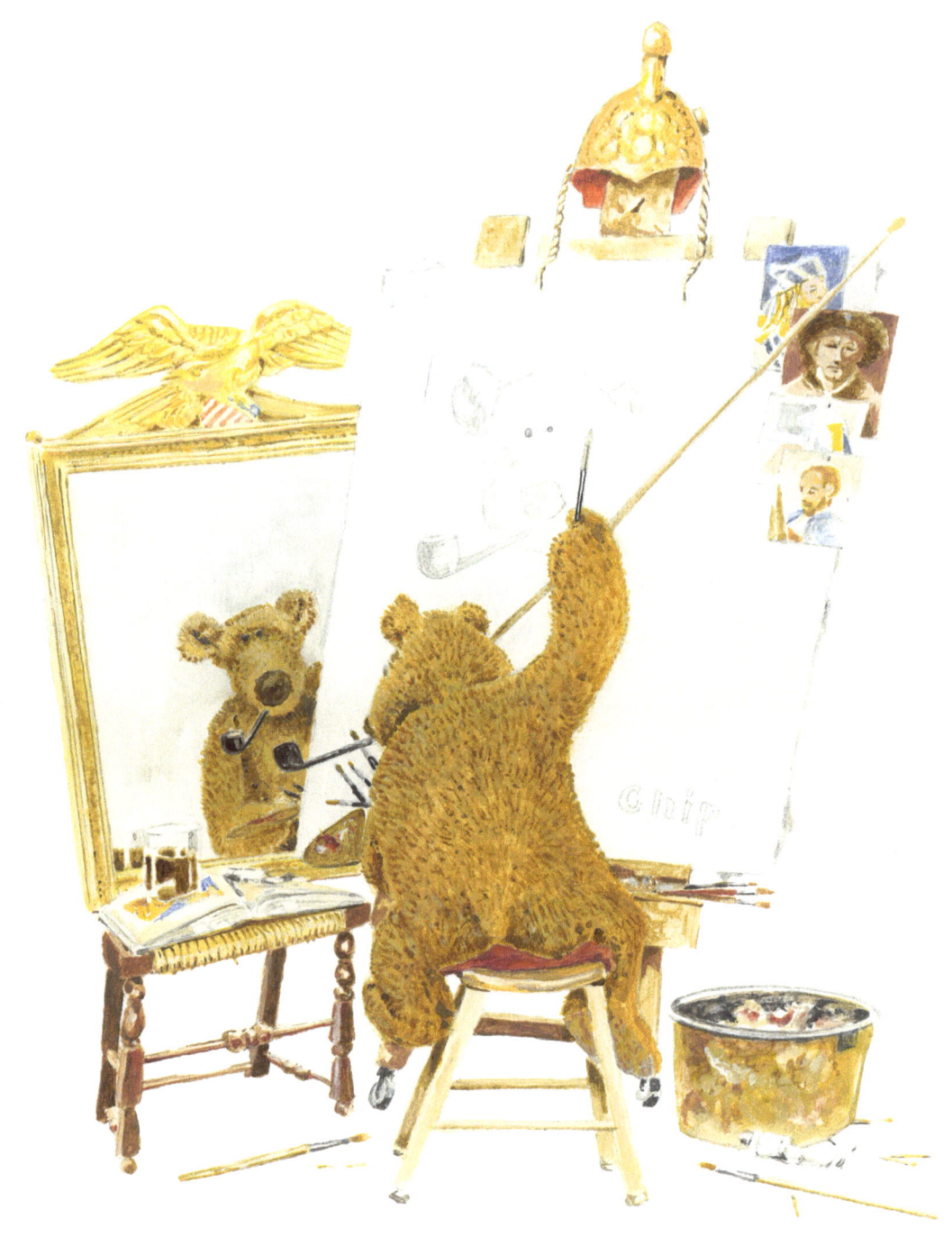

Chip soon became highly sought after for painting portraits; It's no surprise his *Triple Self-Portrait* found its way onto the cover of a popular magazine.

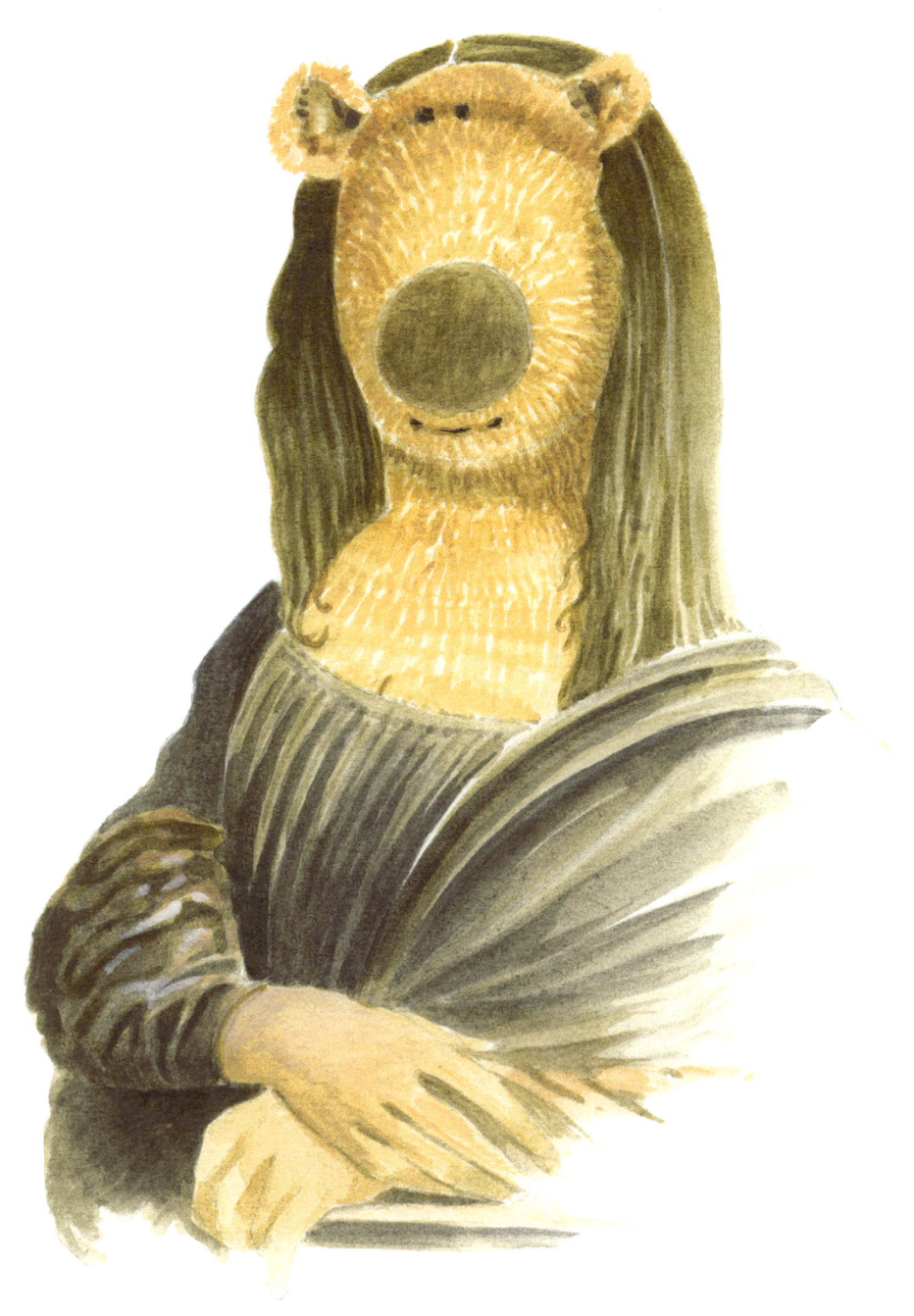

The portrait of his sister, Mona, became famous worldwide...

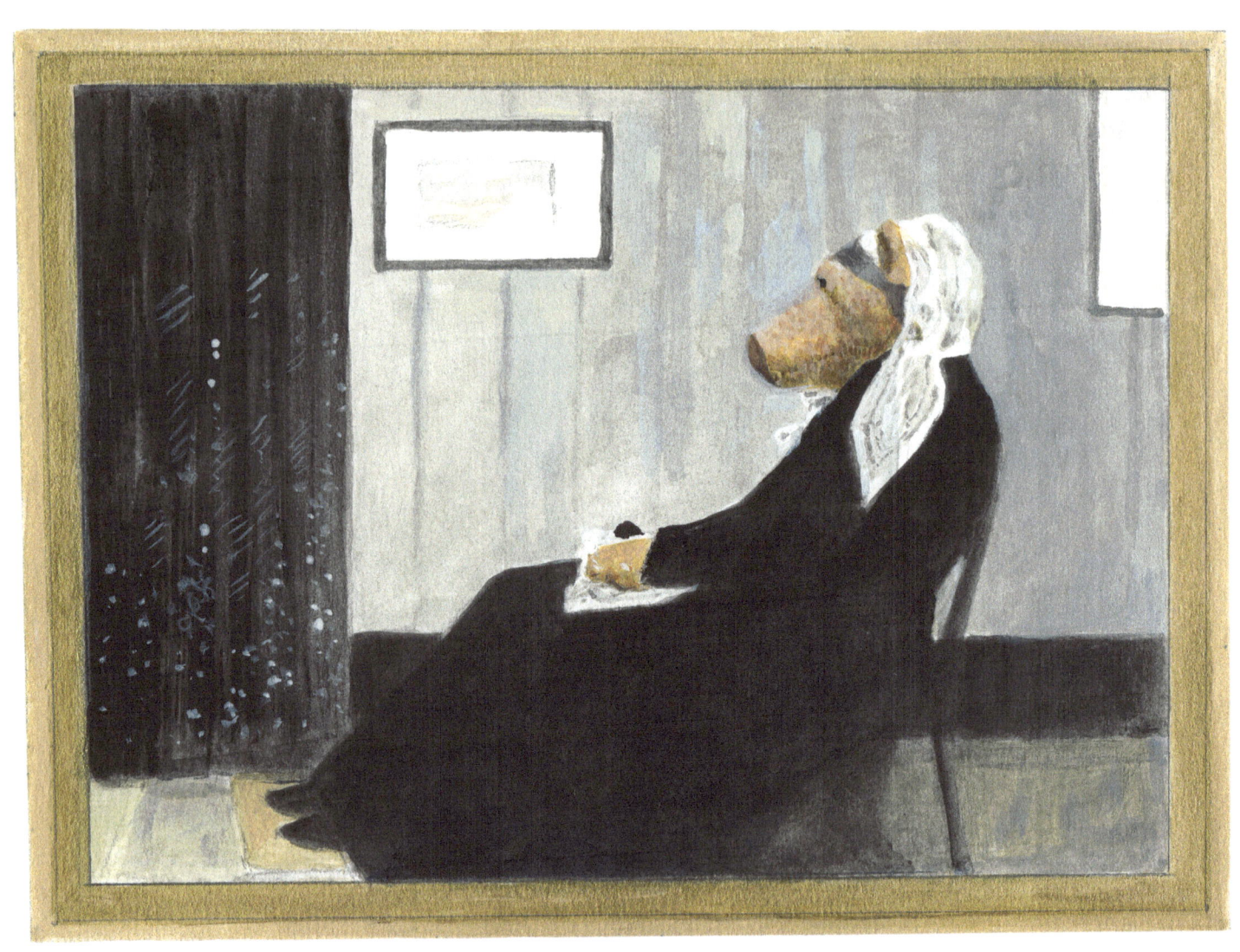

...so did the portrait of his beloved mother.

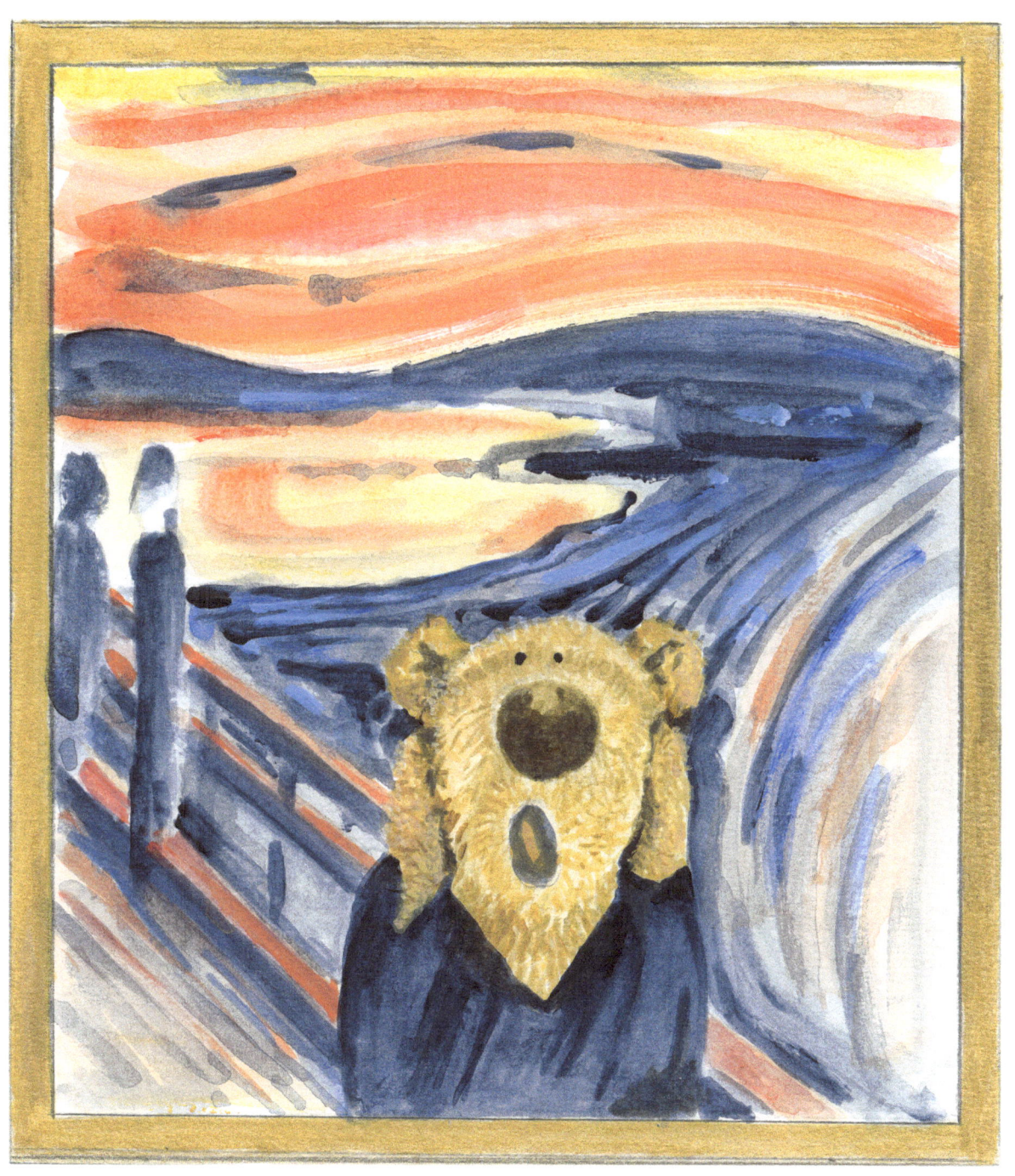

YIKES! was characteristic of his international style.

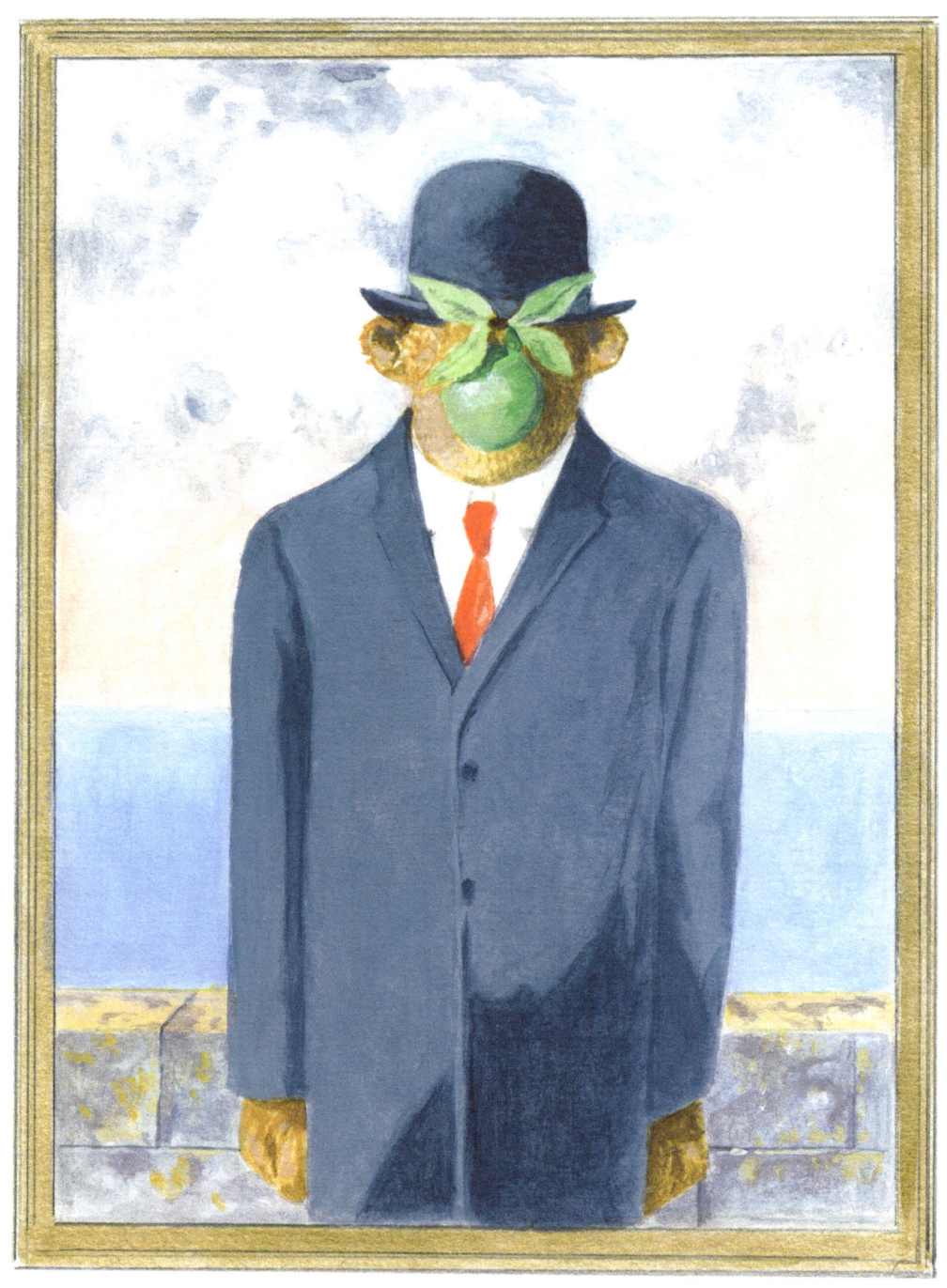

And for a time, a famous Belgian artist informed his choice of subject matter.

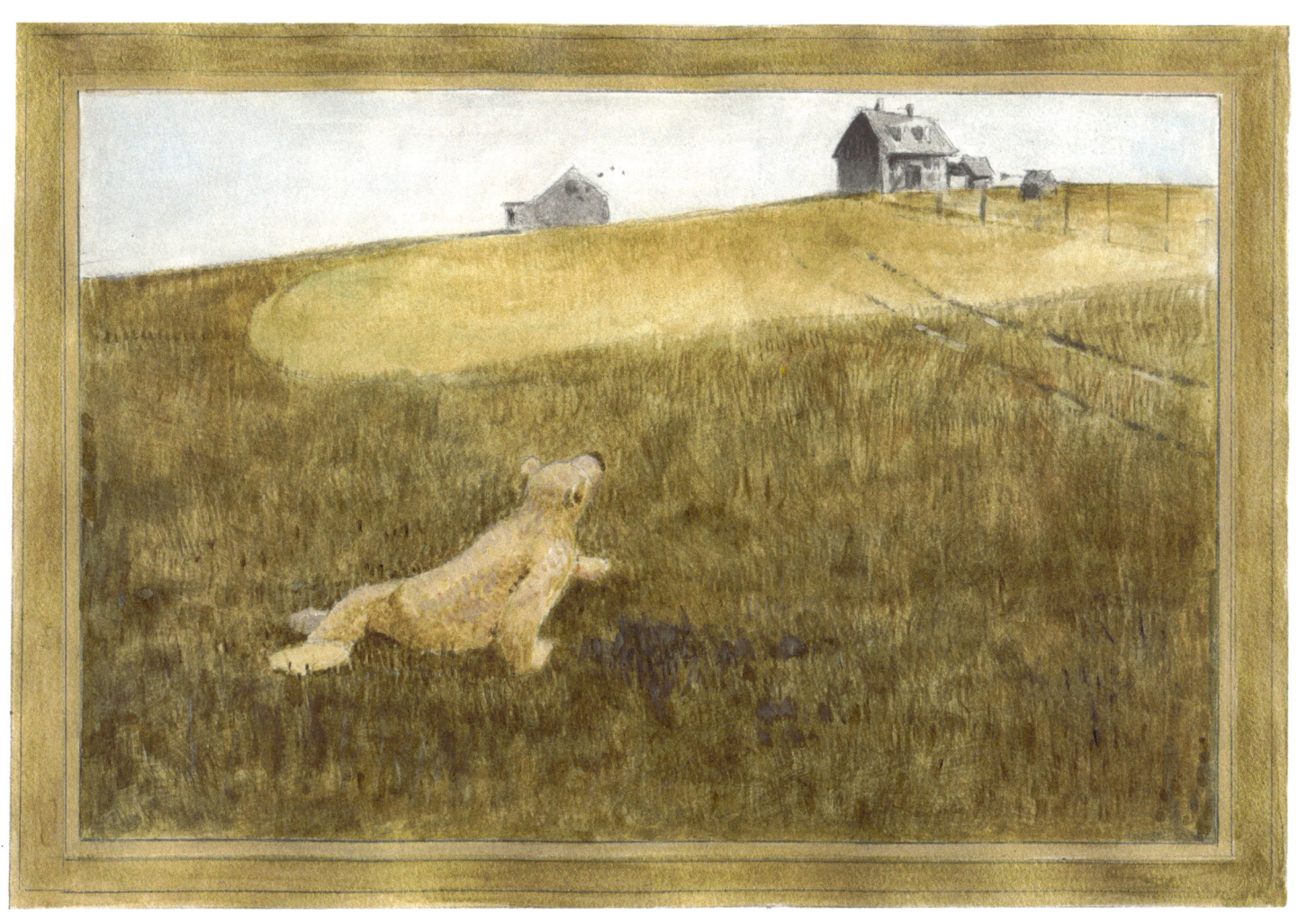

Many have marveled at *Chip's World*, just one of many northern New England paintings he rendered.

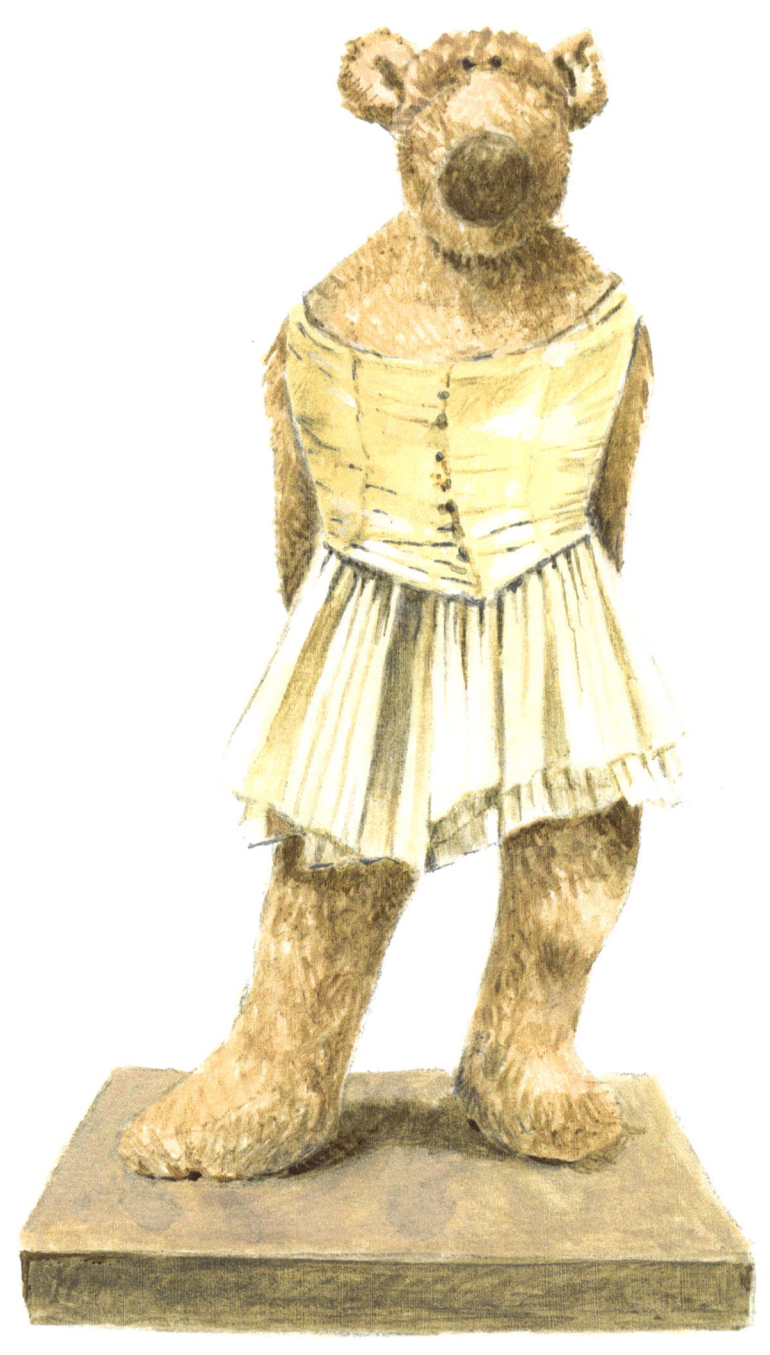

Ballet dancers intrigued him too, inspiring many bronze sculptures now found in most major collections.

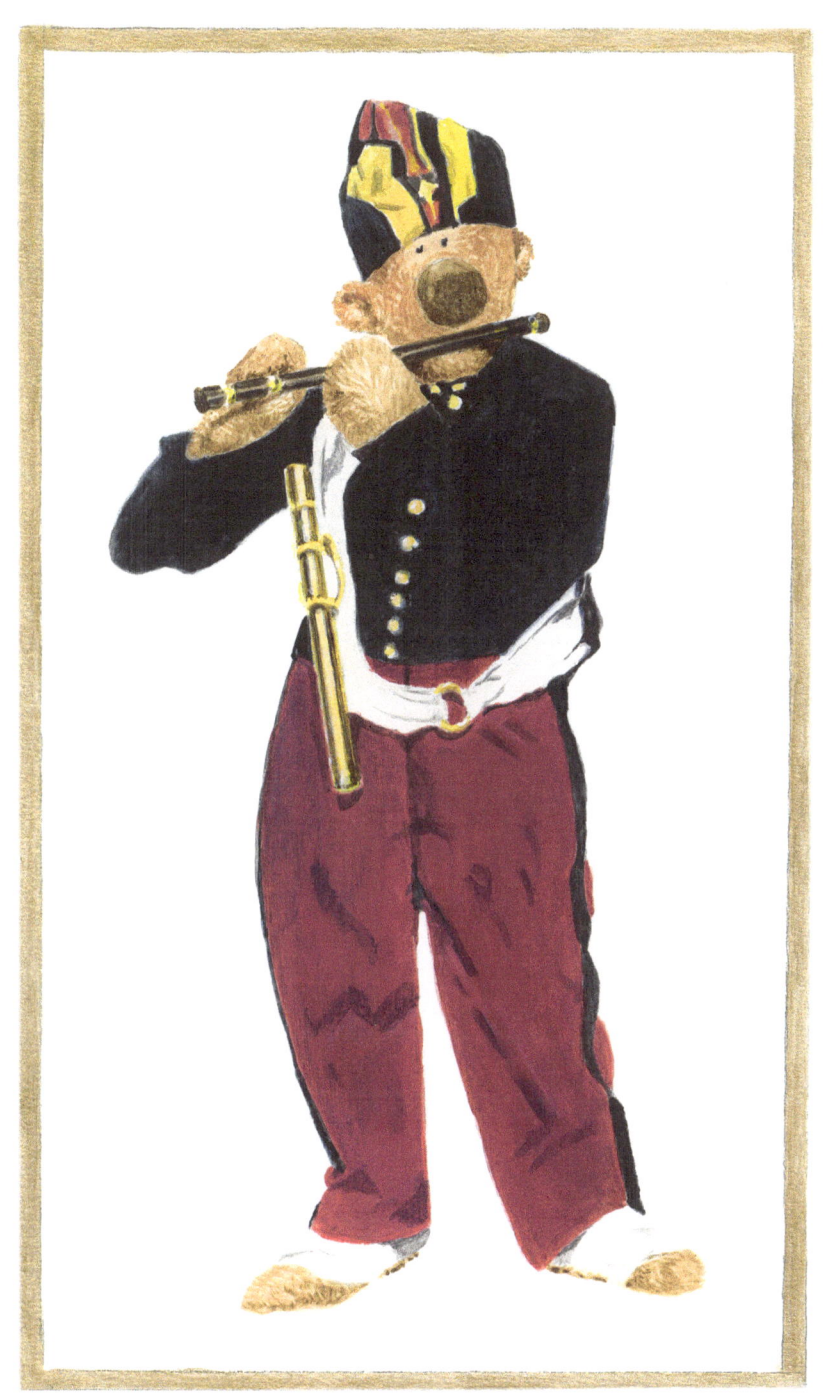

His *Le Fifre* is a breathtaking image.

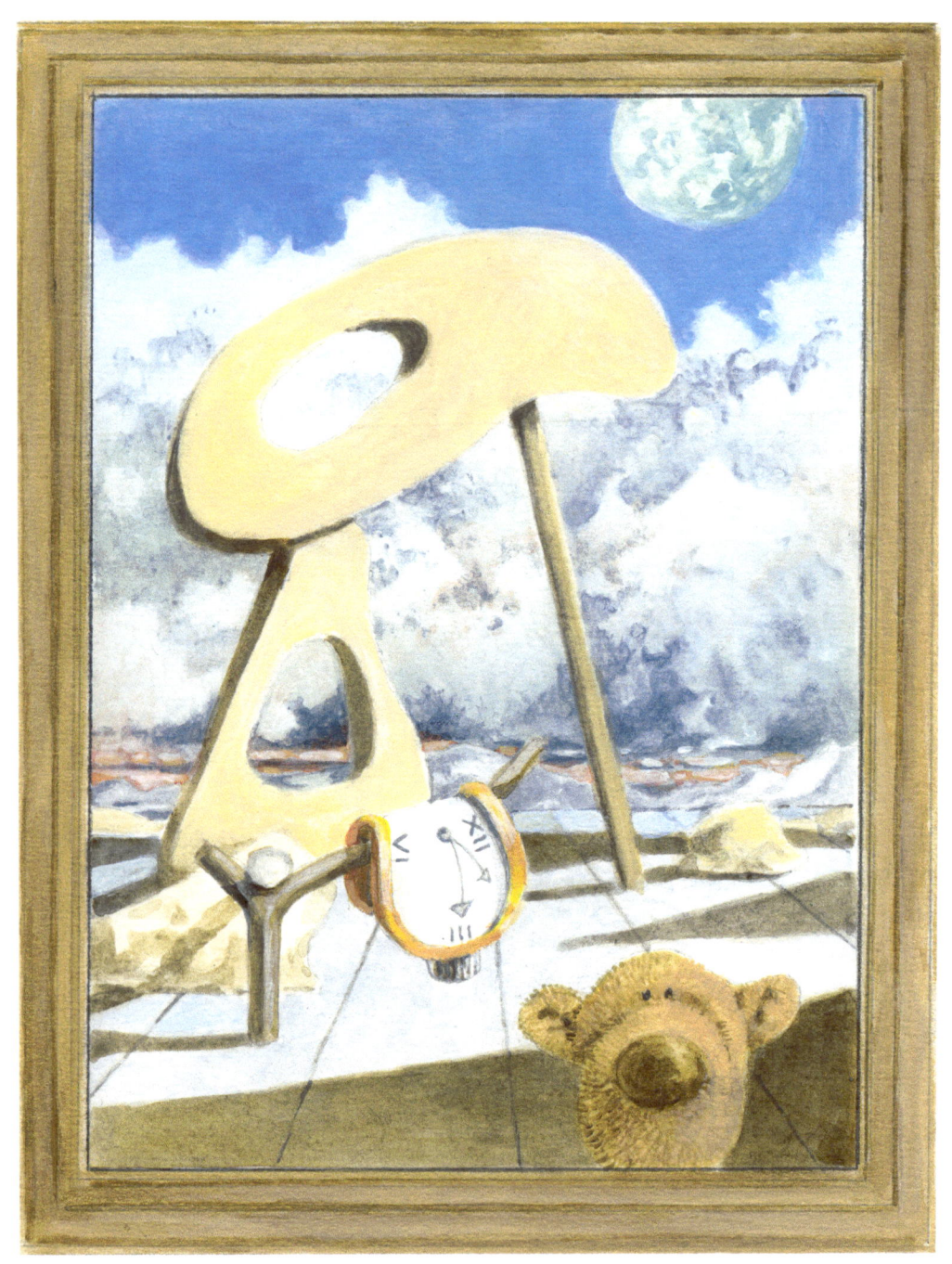

His Spanish sojourn had him dabbling in surrealism. And, if memory serves, he became quite persistent in exploring the nature of time.

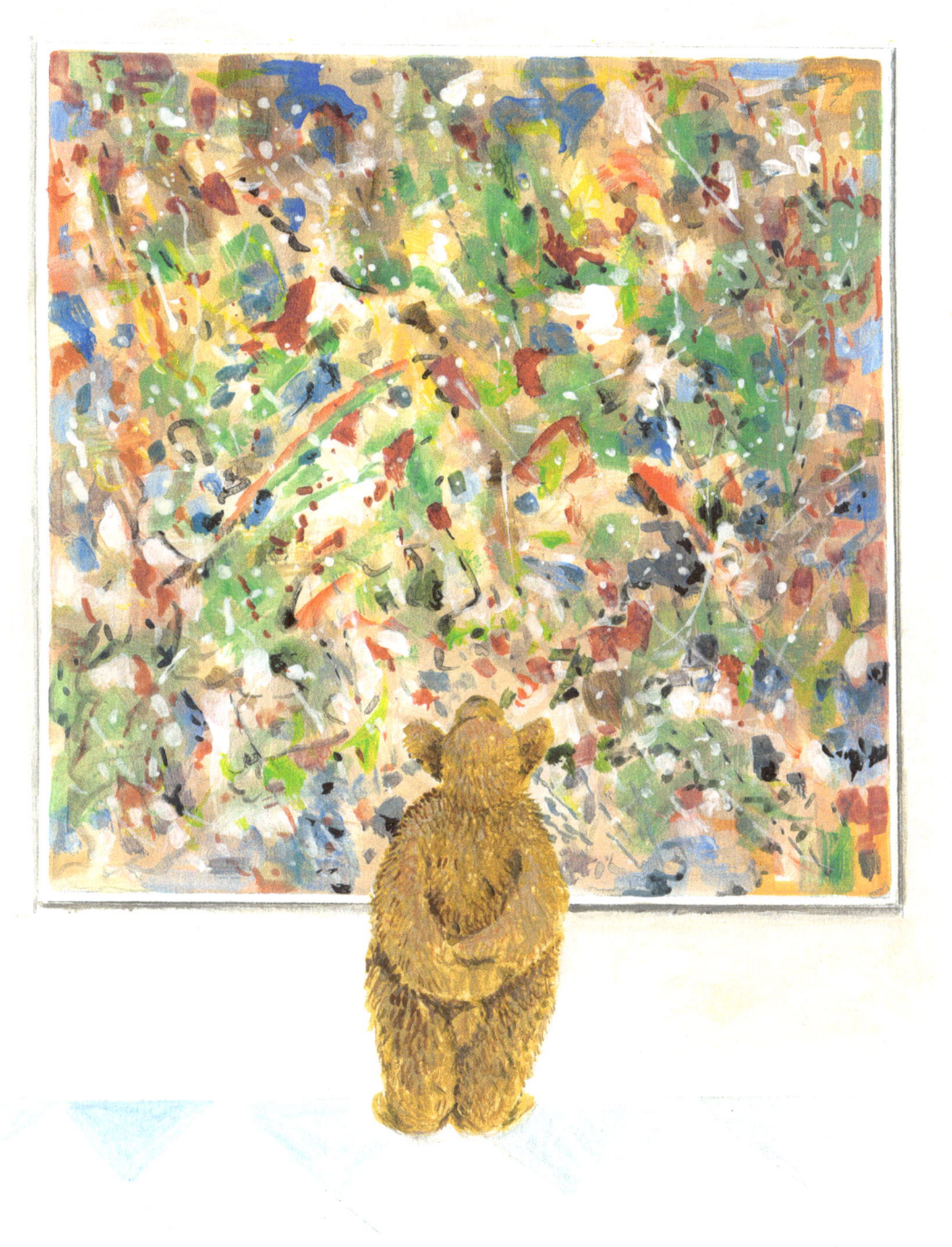

Chip's abstracts grace many a museum wall...

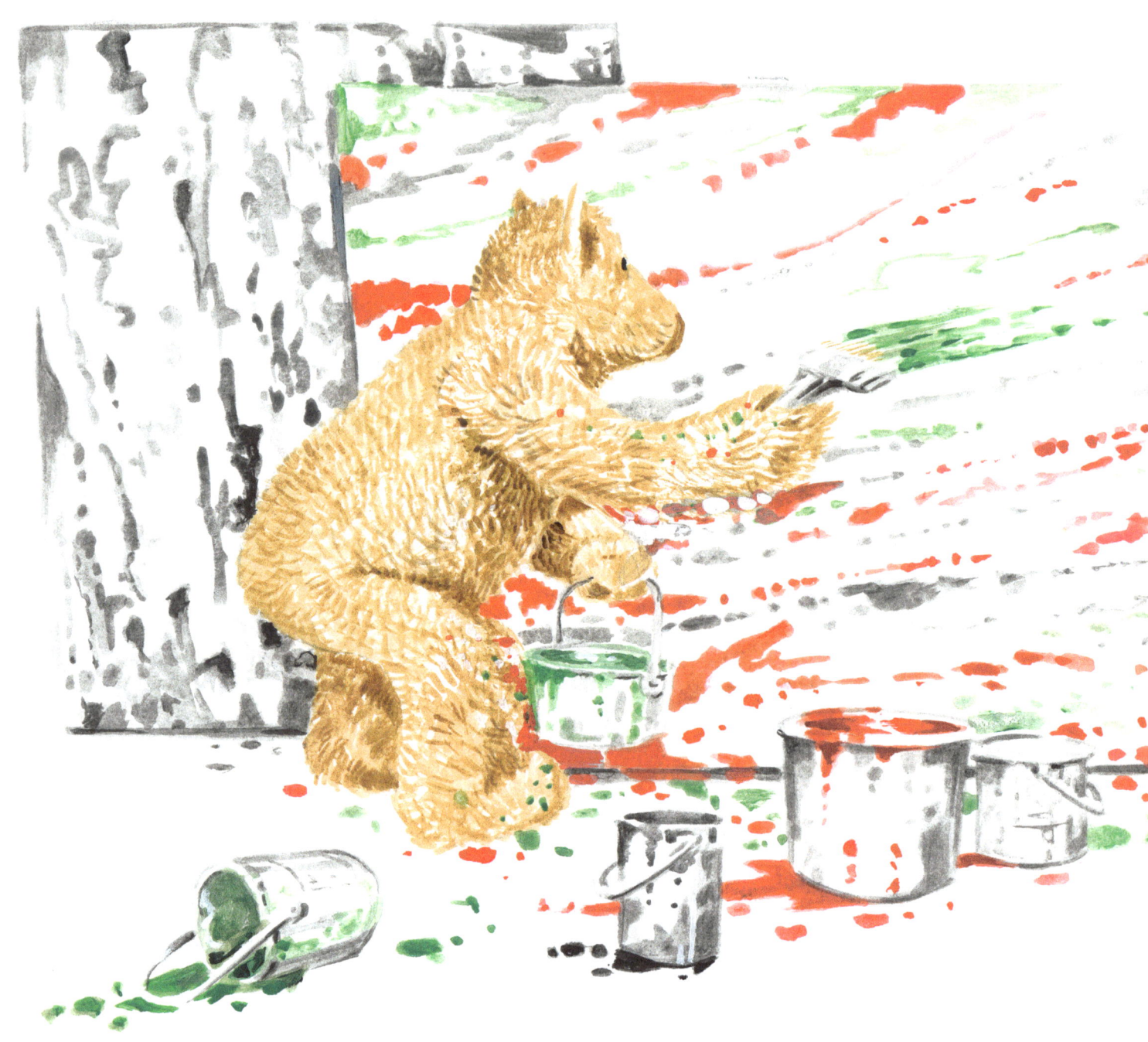

…and his spatter and dribble paintings showcase his exuberance.

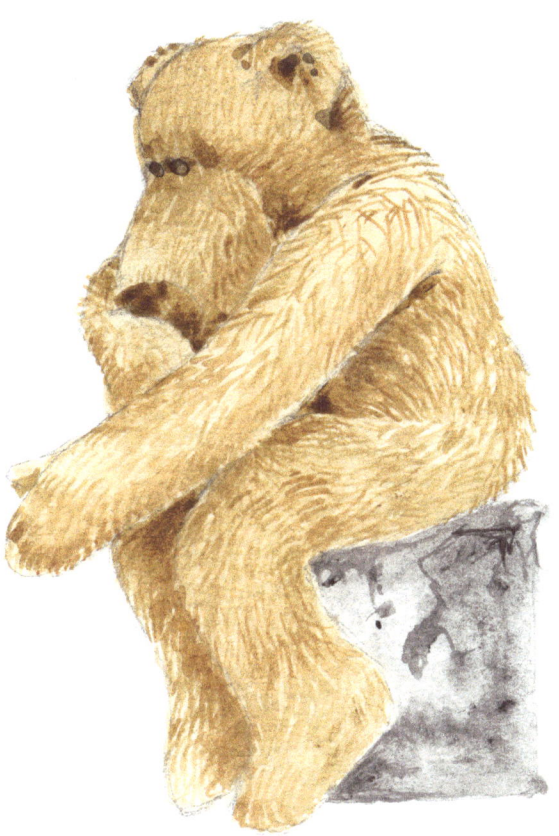

After a lifetime of artistic success, Chip sat down one day and thought "What next?" Reaching out, he was touched by inspiration and heard a voice. Paint a ceiling, it said.

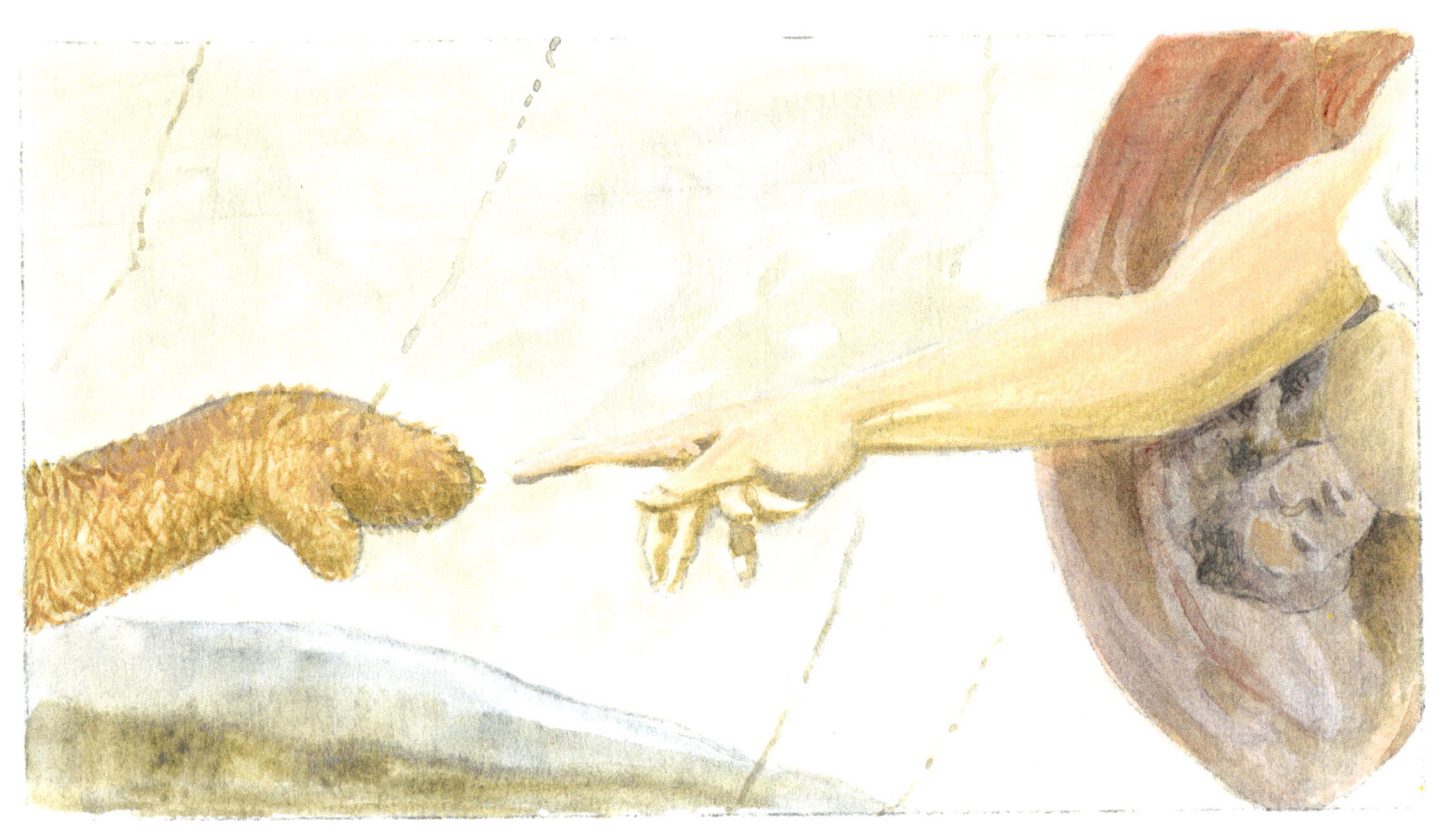

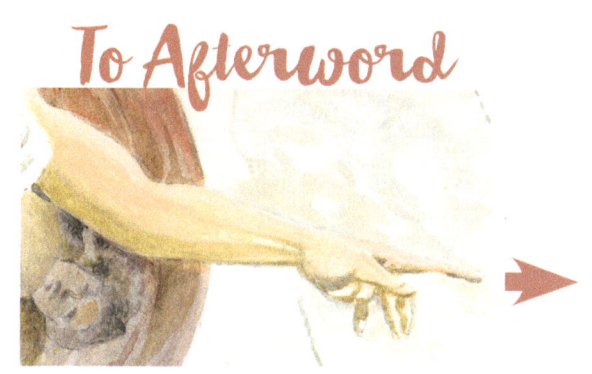

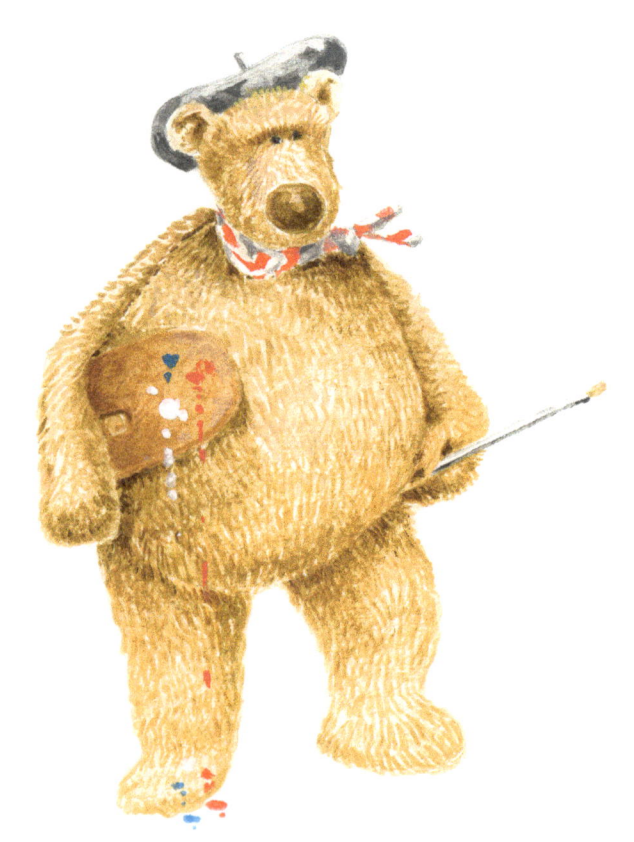

Chip's art is the gold standard. However, the question remains. Did Chip "borrow" from other great and well-known artists, or did they borrow from him? We may never know. Those other artists are:

Page 4: M. C. Escher

Page 8: Norman Rockwell

Page 9: Leonardo da Vinci

Page 10: J. M. Whistler

Page 11: Edvard Munch

Page 12: Rene Magritte

Page 13: Andrew Wyeth

Page 14: Edgar Degas

Page 15: Edouard Manet

Page 16: Salvador Dali(ish)

Page 19: Auguste Rodin

Page 20: Michelangelo Buonarroti

Hmmm...

Well then...if they did the borrowing...shame on them.

The End

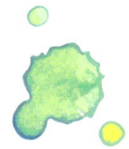

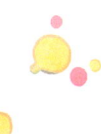

www.ingramcontent.com/pod-product-compliance
Lightning Source LLC
Chambersburg PA
CBHW051839210526
45473CB00005B/1941